AF470877

# Look Behind You!

Other books by the same author include:

SUMMER'S END

Writing as David Merlin:
THE SIMPLE LIFE
THAT BUILT-IN URGE

# Look Behind You!

## An Alphabetical Guide to
## Executive Survival

## David Moreau

*Illustrated by*
Peter Kneebone

Associated Business Programmes
London

Published by
Associated Business Programmes Ltd
17 Buckingham Gate, London S.W.1

First published 1973



This book has been printed in Great Britain
by The Anchor Press Ltd and bound by Wm Brendon & Son Ltd,
both of Tiptree, Essex

ISBN 0 85227 009 7

Justice onwards slowly steals
And Brother Time wounds all heels.

# CONTENTS

# ACKNOWLEDGEMENTS

A few of the essays in this book have appeared in modified form in *The Director*, the journal of the Institute of Directors, and I am very grateful to the Editors, Eric Foster and George Bull, for permission to reprint them here.

I would also like to thank Peter Kneebone for crystallising in pin-sharp and economical detail the figments of my managerial imagination.

One of the most noticeable features of long-serving senior executives in big companies is that, although they often grumble about their lot, they nearly all show a doggy willingness to roll over and expose their soft underparts to the jackboot if the company decides to mistreat them.

It also occurs to me that some of the big corporations demand from their senior servants a degree of serfdom that has scarcely been seen since the days of Greece and Rome. Unpaid overtime is taken for granted. Car size is as effectively restricted as dress was in the days of the Sumptuary Laws. Office size and carpeted area are laid down to the inch. Pension schemes induce increasing terror in ageing executives in case they should be cut off from the pittance that will make their declining days tolerable. Management by Objectives makes sure that a man's own desperate promises made at the beginning of the year keep him on a treadmill that turns ever faster. Sensitivity and $T$ sessions ensure that there is no privacy left even in a man's personality—every worthwhile eccentricity he has is dragged out and booted about by his colleagues, subordinates and superiors. Graduates of business administration sit shaking their heads at the boss's incomprehension, quietly carrying in the barrels for the Gunpowder Plot that will ultimately lift him into oblivion. Thinking of these two factors, first the stiff-upper-lipped defencelessness of the typical executive and second the thinly disguised slavery that he endures while waiting for the bang of the humane killer, decided me to put these notes together.

It is customary to recite one's qualifications for showering others with gratuitous advice, particularly about so grave a matter as their survival. I will confine myself to saying that I have seen quite a few rubber aprons put on in corporate charnel houses, and sometimes the sound of the bolt gun has left me deaf for days.

I did an accidental job of market research on the subject of company assassins when I wrote a piece about them for *The Director* a couple of years ago. It was taken up widely by the media. At the time I was thinking mainly of the two hundred or so directors who are done to death by their colleagues or holding companies annually, but it was obvious from the letters which came in that quite apart from business, thousands of people live in fear of being rejected by organisations as diverse as the BBC, Government, political parties, their golf clubs, and even voluntary bodies. I used to say that changing your job, willingly or unwillingly, was a healthy appeal to your flexibility. Now that I see more clearly the connection with human loneliness, and the pride and self-confidence that keep an individual together, I am not so sure.

## ADVERTISING

I once knew a man whose car, camera, mistress, books, whisky and general high standard of living came from the advertising agency with whom he spent a quarter of a million pounds of the appropriation his company generously provided him with as their advertising manager. As far as I know, they never found out; he just rioted his way to an early death. He was, however, the exception. Most people who get into the hedonistic grasp of a supplier get shopped sooner or later. It is not only that their prosperity becomes too evident and excites denunciatory jealousy, but also that, as always with the sudden yawning of Ali Baba's cave, the over-stimulated human being to whom it happens gets both greedy and careless.

Although in varying degrees a regrettably frequent side-effect of contact with the devil-may-care advertising world, luxury is far from the only danger. Honest over-spending is probably just as good evidence for those bent on homicide, particularly in new companies with foreign principals who look in boardrooms in Frankfurt, Milan and New York at a cumulative debt run up by their British subsidiary on such a scale that it will doubtfully be paid off by the year 2000.

Then there is the expensive advertising campaign that falls flat on its back because it is ill-judged, potty, uses last year's trendy jargon, tries to sell a worthless product that should never have been launched anyway, or, in spite of being expensive, is also bafflingly dull. Most marketing men love their autonomy, as do most advertising managers. But if the sugar cane around them is rustling with company dacoits, it is only sensible to do one of two things; if you think you are making a colossal mistake, call a committee of your probable assassins and get them to sign the minutes that list their names at the top as approving. Or, if you have a chairman or a director who can be identified in writing with your potentially sinking ship, do it. Chopping those responsible for unsuccessful launches and sales campaigns is a blood sport which is going to grow in popularity now that the commercial seas are dotted with the desperately swimming figures of shipwrecked sales executives. So if you are likely to join them, make sure that the ship's captain and a large slice of the crew are there as well.

## *AGEING*

Who is currently the most on-turning film star for girls in their late teens? Steve McQueen. How old is he? About forty. How old were the first seven men on the moon? About forty. How old was the Italian co-driver of the 1,000 H.P. *Lady Nara*, who after saving the lives of his driver and mechanic in the gale-tossed 1971 *Daily Express* powerboat race, went on to win the event? Sixty-one. How old was Sir Francis Chichester when he sailed single-handed around the world? Mid-sixties.

I mention these miscellaneous facts because they show that, with modern attitudes to diet and keeping fit, and with medicine increasingly preserving the ageing human body in trim, the precise chronographic age is becoming unimportant. The oldest executive I ever took on was over sixty, and he did the job he was employed for admirably. As a hangover from earlier eras, you will still find men who dread their fortieth birthday as if from that moment on they will go into a moral, physical and sexual decline from which nothing will arrest them. They are already half-defeated long before the actual accusations are voiced that they have lost their abdominal fire, ceased to be flexible, forgotten how to transmit youthful enthusiasm, or show signs of failing memory and decision-taking power.

Remember the men whom I listed at the beginning. They know that a mature physique will keep going when the rest have stopped. That a judgement that has lived through every known situation at least once before will not be panicked by its sudden reappearance. And that the greatest single form of attraction that any man can exercise on both men and women is the confidence that comes from power and success, irrespective of age.

## *ASSASSINS*

Nasty accidents can happen to any senior executive, whether he is aged twenty-eight or seventy, and he can find himself looking for a job. But the typical assassination victim that I am thinking of has been a director for five years or more, is aged forty to sixty, and is earning more than five thousand pounds a year. He has probably passed his Level of Incompetence in Peter's terms, but then so have most other senior people from the Prime Minister down, and Society continues nevertheless to function somehow. I have a supplementary theory to the Peter one anyway—that the human brain is only suited to sustain control and leadership over groups about the size of the itinerant tribes that have formed the units of human society for 98 per cent of the three-quarters of a million years that human beings have been around to date. With bigger units, whether countries, organisations like ICI, or even large towns, the problems are too complex, hydra-headed and numerous for any human mind to grasp and resolve them. The solution is obviously a self-programming computer, and eventually one may get the edifying spectacle of one ambitious young computer politically assassinating another older, more established one.

No one in high office is safe because a determined opponent who has little to lose can always show that his victim has one of three fatal flaws; he is either: (1) Incompetent; (2) Insufficiently trendy in management terms, or (3) Over-involved with either grog or birds, or both.

So what can be done? First, you must know your enemies. Identifying these can be quite exciting in itself. Second, they must be within striking distance of you, so that they are certainly earning at least £2,500 a year. Third, they will be political animals, so that they are unlikely to be doctors, scientists or engineers. They are likely to be accountants (if a business is in economic trouble, the chairman always reaches for the faculty which is supposed to understand the figure problem, even if it does not understand the human one), marketing men, lawyers or social scientists. The people, in fact, who cause social disorder everywhere. Your assassin will probably be between twenty-eight and forty; most likely in his late thirties and haunted by the prospect of reaching the imagined cut-off age of forty without making it. He may be a heavy smoker as a sign of an ingrowing aggression. He may have more children than he can afford, which is both a possible indication of recklessness and an economic spur to being a regicide. His wife may well be an ugly shrew, which is a motivation to earn more so that he can afford the dolly birds that his horrible homecomings at night make him long for. He may go suddenly pale with anger and frustration when talking to you because he is convinced that you are an old twit, and everything that you do that concerns him is a botched job. In a baboon pack his pent-up fury would make him sink his fangs into your throat, but with you the murder in his heart has to be canalised into plotting your downfall by easy stages.

Looking round your executive committee, there are only relatively few demeanours to be seen. The stable, well-adjusted, contented executive, making sensible and sparing contributions. You have nothing to fear from him. The honest, volatile man whose anger and humour succeed one another like April weather. He is probably all right. The sycophant, who may have BO as well because being so silkily nice is a strain on anyone. He is not likely to be your assassin, but he may well be his henchman. Then the assassin himself. He probably disagrees overtly or tacitly with almost everything you say, sometimes without actually being able to suggest an alternative course. He is probably either very small or very large, particularly if you are of medium size. In fact, whatever size you are, he is most likely to be the opposite—thin when you are fat, or dwarfish if you are giraffe-like. He may have resigned from a previous company, and a mysterious exit—particularly if he was paid real money to get off the premises—must always make you suspect that he has taken a vow that next time it will be someone other than himself who will be humiliated.

Men who used to take part in some really violent sport, such as rugby or boxing, may subsequently have difficulty in getting rid of their aggressive urges in the harmless placidity of ambling round the golf course, and they may become intriguers in their need for excitement. Immature men require to be watched —a friend of mine was suddenly shot as a highly successful chairman of a large and profitable firm acquired by a paternalistic group. His assassin from the wings, a portly character, gave an interview to a major Sunday paper in which—although over sixty—he spewed out a description of all his own numerous talents like a small boy trying to impress at a new school. The fellow had obviously never matured enough to develop real loyalty to his former colleague.

Finally in identifying authentic threats round you, it may in fact be best to rely on the basic hunch mechanism which we have from our savage forbears.

If a man avoids your eye, stops talking and shuffles when you suddenly appear, takes uncharacteristically pragmatic action when you are away, or writes memos to any superiors with copy to you about things that he could perfectly well discuss with you, watch him like a hunting stoat; and assume that he is guilty until he proves himself innocent, preferably by resigning.

## BIRDS

Not long ago the journal *Nature* published an article by an anonymous scientist, working alone on a remote British island during the week, who had observed that the prospect of a weekend at home with his girlfriend made his beard grow twice as fast on Fridays. In fact it is a physiological commonplace that the presence of an attractive member of the opposite sex turns up the metabolic rate of practically everything including the production of male hormones, blood pressure and blood sugar. It is logical, therefore, that the kind of muscular entrepreneur who is often to be found near the top of an ant-heap will at the very least feel the need (or need the feel) of two *au pair* girls. The male who makes convenient arrangements at home is almost certainly safe, provided of course that his lawful spouse is not on the Board of Directors as well. It is when he has to have a similar regular stimulus during office hours that the trouble starts. This is for four reasons:

(1) Female company is incomparably habituating, particularly to the older male and a really inspiring relationship in the office will almost certainly end up with grapples on the interviewing couch. It is then only a question of time before someone—even if only the cleaner—catches him at it.

(2) Even a boss who is a male virgin will, given time, collect a mythological allegation round him that he has had someone (male or female) after an office party, and similar legends. So that one who really does so is very unlikely to avoid the throbbing of the jungle telegraph. This is all part of being a Dominant Ape, as many male figures in public life have repeatedly found over the last twenty years.

(3) Hell, as the ancient adage has it, does not harbour anything so vindictively twisted as a woman who has been traded in for a new model. I knew one once who rang a managing director and insisted on speaking to him while he was chairing a board meeting, screaming at him that she was pregnant in a voice intended to echo round the panelling. She wasn't really. She just wanted to get her own back for being supplanted. So remember, no matter how beautiful your relationship may seem with your graceful new personal assistant, a time may come when spite makes her ratty enough to betray you several times over.

(4) Last, and deadliest of all, remember the sexual

jealousy that burns in the solar plexus of young men of all ages. Say, for example, that you are regularly but secretly having a bird on the staff, and a younger executive asks her out to dinner. She refuses. He feels spurned, and investigates her indifference with the same mad devotion to detail as people show when doing their expenses. Finally he suspects you. I tell you, if he can possibly arrange it, your days are numbered.

Deliberately here I have ignored the situation of the female executive, first, because she is rare as a hetero-sexual problem, second, because I have never seen from the inside the tangles that female executives get into, and third, because, except in extreme and Amazonian cases, it is always the aggressive male who has set the pace and therefore has the last chance to stop things before they become lethal.

I have stated the problem, but not given the solution. This is for the obvious reason; there is none. Naturally I could preach at you like some otiose (and probably hypogenital) Father of the Church, saying that you should not touch the office birds under any circumstances. I remember Sir Frederick Catherwood suggesting in his embarrassingly holy little book *The Christian in Industry* that executives should 'eschew the dance' at the Christmas party so as not to risk office entanglements. The infantility of the rest of this book does not necessarily make this statement invalid. But perhaps the best advice one can give to the rabidly oversexed executive is to keep his private life vivid enough for him to be able to manage the few hours of daily famine that continence at the office will represent. The expense of your second *au pair* girl will be much less than it will cost you if an assassin manages to shop you with a chairman who regards office fornication as a loath-some capital offence.

## *BUSTED FLUSHES, MEN WHO ARE*

Zigzagging about in every industry there are a few Busted Flushes who have been fired with full military honours from companies every few years, survive, and bob up in another company only weeks later with even more impressive ranks than before. Such people —I know some spectacular cases—are both dangerous and instructive. Dangerous because they are certainly incompetent and will surround themselves with even lower-grade individuals in order to make their survival more likely. So that if one comes into your outfit as general manager and you have the misfortune to be a highly competent subordinate, your future is in jeopardy. You may have to camouflage yourself with a healthy dimness, and allow his drunkenness or fumbling to pass wholly unremarked.

But men with such records of repeated and imperial failure are highly instructive to study because *they have survived*. How do they do it? First, they always know a lot of people in high places in their industry and make sure that they keep their acquaintances in good repair, often with meals at the current company's expense. Second, apart from being grossly incapable, they often appear to be very nice chaps—jovial, lovable, funny, considerate. If you really get close to them you may find that their concern for survival makes them sud-denly narrow-eyed as they look for a bolt-hole when any rough-stuff breaks out, but this is understandable, even praiseworthy. And if you frequent their company you will sometimes find the questions that they ask—when is your wife's birthday, for example, so that they can send her some flowers—distinctly exaggerated. And if you have the misfortune not to survive at some stage, your relations will suddenly cool to freezing point. They do not like to be associated with failure; it may make survival more difficult next time.

## *BOREDOM*

As you get higher up the structure *ennui*, my friends, is your number one enemy, the likely cause of most or all of the other scrapes that you get into—whether lasciviousness, gormandising or neglect of your functions. Human beings, like their own muscles, are turned on and grow strong through use. This is the tragedy of the unused human machines in most old peoples' homes. And, as soldiers and airmen in the last war learned to their bitter cost, while hidden for incredibly dull and inactive weeks at a time in safe addresses in occupied towns like Paris, boredom dulls the sense of danger and encourages folly.

The plain fact is that, when you reach the rank of managing director, your day has no structure. Possibly you went to a public school where you got used to a regular rhythm of games, work and breaks. At university it was somewhat similar. Then, as you toiled through the company's infrastructure, your boss largely dictated your comings and goings.

Suddenly you seem to be free. Nobody can complain overtly if you turn up at ten o'clock every day, get up to God-knows-what for two hours every lunch hour, and only stay in the office for an hour or two at the end of the day because you have a tryst there.

Analysis of chief executives as I have known them shows broadly four types of individual:

(1) The highly-disciplined, well-motivated man who has known how to hold on to a few vital company functions, convenes the right number of top meetings, and is widely respected for his sparing and sensible interventions in company activities. Far from needing or being able to do anything for him, I apologise for even having mentioned him in this meretricious work.

(2) Next down comes a capable, well-organised man who feels that his role is particularly to act as a top level PR man for his company. He knows everybody, in the City as elsewhere, and spends a lot of time lunching and in minor public relations matters. His activity in the company's various departments tends to be rather erratic— he makes irruptions into their work, sometimes of a rather irascible nature, and possibly lays a lot of emphasis on gentlemanly behaviour. His company will probably prosper if he has chosen his team carefully. But he may have problems if simultaneously his production goes to pot, a powerful competitor breaks out, his wife leaves him for a poet and the R and D goes completely sterile; this is because sheer lack of day-to-day experience with departmental activities in the company will prevent him from master-minding skilful and precise remedial action.

(3) The man who is too small intellectually to occupy the top position in a company. Or too

old. Or too old-fashioned. Or too specialised. Or a combination of these. If he is really conscientious he will battle on for years with an inadequate sense of priorities which in turn will mean that he will infuriate the people under him by giving fanatical attention to small things which he happens to understand, while failing utterly to deal with company-threatening issues because he is either afraid of these or quite unable to recognise them. Often he will be a nice man, with an appealing personality when he is not angry and afraid at his own inadequacy. Because of the tiny percentage of really competent leaders in any field that are born every year, this is probably the commonest single type of top company executive. Most of us know one; but I hope that this is not a thumbnail picture of you, because if it is you will be a sitter for a hard-headed assassin.

(4) The grotesquely self-indulgent who boozes limitlessly, has birds from eight o'clock in the morning on, adjourns meetings so that he can stay in bed, is last into the office and first out; plays golf when the House is debating the future of his industry, and goes to Ascot the day before that modern World Eisteddfod, his international planning meeting.

The odd thing about the last sort of chap is that he almost certainly has a drunken and dissipated charisma which gives him a power of survival, which in some cases becomes legendary. Once upon a time, there was a minister and politician who staggered belching through reception after reception. He might well have survived if his Prime Minister hadn't been rather jealous of him anyway. Many of these people, far from being incompetent, are actually men of courage and great ability if they give themselves a chance. It is just that fifteen minutes of thinking about what they are really supposed to do bores them so desperately, that they would much rather risk disgrace than deprive themselves of the hours of stolen glee that result from doing something pleasurable but dreadful.

Such people, lurching forward on a raft of their own charm and ability, can often survive for years before the lashings finally part and the sharks get them. And God bless them, I say; there are enough whey-faced corporate courtiers about to make these few splendid buffoons indispensable.

## COMPASSION

As all parents notice, children, like savages, have little or no ability to feel Compassion. The civilised ability to feel acutely for other people mainly grows on us in our late teens, often producing an efflorescence of transitory concern for underdogs during the University years. The odd citizen continues to feel compassion as an adult, and he or she generally ends up as a geriatrician, nurse, social worker or (in perversely rich cases) full-time philanthropist. A well-known professional Compassionist used to parade his grieving heart across the columns of the women's magazines until his death just a few years ago—I am not giving his name because he is a principle rather than an identity. According to a distinguished columnist, this particular experienced sympathiser used frequently to burst into tears at his own plight if a scurvy editor failed to offer him a suitably high fee. His fountain of sad Compassion helped him to die a rich man, having started with nothing.

His case makes an important point. The struggle to survive is now so energy-consuming that most people have little drive left over to feel practical and disinterested compassion. In other words, if you want to make someone merciful or sympathetic towards you, nine times out of ten there has to be something for them in this exercise of putting themselves in your shoes. Not always—I know a case of an American company executive who thought that an injustice had been done to the murdered manager of a European subsidiary of theirs, and who continued to say so loudly to his own peril at many of the executive committee meetings until his own future began to darken. But such quixotism is rare (see *Lose, What You May, if Assassinated*).

So, if you are in reasonable fear of the knife, the name of the game is sudden indispensability to someone so that he cares. Who? Preferably the hand that switches on the Psychologist-Exorcist, i.e. the chairman or managing director. If you feel able to stoop that low, you can become one of the lovable creeps that I cover under *Odours*, although if you are in positive danger, it is unlikely that you are inadequate enough to melt into their scene. And, in the long run, you would find death preferable to being so nauseously Nice. Well? A one word answer: Profit. You are the financial controller? You stay in your office for a few evenings (make sure that this is widely reported) drawing up a plan to slash overheads, shut factories, discharge workers, showing the tempting savings that will be possible. Remember that Compassion nowadays is a highly selective phenomenon. (How often did the professional Compassionist I mentioned at the beginning weep for the dying journals from which he asked such large sums?) So that if someone else is going to get hurt while you curry some concrete sympathy for yourself, that is not your present concern.

Let us assume that you are a sales manager, reporting to a marketing director who is moving in on you for the kill. You might ask for an audience with the managing director and reveal your plan to double sales with half the sales force by redeploying them in areas which can be more effectively worked. You can even indicate to him (with the abundant production of facts) that it is disagreement with your marketing director over the desirability of actually reducing your empire which has produced the current potentially fatal dispute.

You may think that my suggestions are wild; but I tell you as a chief executive of some years battle-hardening, nothing implores your Compassion more than someone from beneath who voluntarily comes out with a seemingly sound plan to ease your hard and stony road to profitability, particularly if (and this is the clever bit) it appears to result in actual reduction in the scope or responsibilities of the Compassion generator.

## *CITY, KEEPING THE LOVE OF THE*

In a book by John Brooks called *Once in Golconda* the following passage appears:

The leaders of Wall Street were among the first Organisation men—selfish, opinionated, and, bizarrely, thinking of themselves as gentlemen. In the beginning consisting almost exclusively of Old Eastern Gentile stock, they were not overly bright, but had a kind of stubborn shrewdness. Consummate snobs, they were remarkably ignorant about art, literature, music, history, world affairs apart from business, theoretical economics—just about everything except the matter in hand, and sports. They were unabashedly preoccupied with money, and had no ambitions except to become richer and more socially prominent.

Things are not that terrible in the City of London. There is a dominant public school influence, combined with an ex-military whiff of men who had a good war, but you can easily find very cultured, generous and even unconventional men who dispose of power and large sums of money. What you have to remember is that the financial mandarins, regardless of their personal width of character, must protect not only their own monetary interests but also those of a lot of others. They will therefore:

(1) Be chary of sudden prosperity, showy marketing techniques that remind them of John Bloom and Bernie Cornfeld, and schemes that are sold as having no disadvantages. Since the days of the South Sea Bubble, mature City men have learned to sniff all round a new proposition with the same care as an elephant that fears there may be native assegais downwind.

(2) Deprecate personal boastfulness. This is not just because the creaking nineteenth-century manliness cult of their public schools bars it, but be-

cause people to whom the need to boast is a real compulsion are doubtfully suitable for high command or financial office because they are immature in judgement and, often, have a fatally low opinion of themselves. And a man who needs to talk about himself and labour his own cleverness can easily be flattered so that he does not even realise that he is being manoeuvred into a losing position by an appeal to his vanity.

(3) Dislike erratic behaviour. Although companies whose shares yo-yo about in time with their behaviour are useful to speculators, the great mass of investors—including institutional ones like the Prudential and the ICI Pension Fund—have bought a particular share because they are a safe, progressive investment that does not require constant attention. And the consistent upward trend means that the minimum of servicing is required to defeat the steady rot in money value.

(4) Use the very effective grapevine in organisations like Lloyds and the Stock Exchange. Men are actually worse gossips than women, and when a large number are collected together with intermittent periods of slack trade and boredom, a lot of talk is generated. It therefore gets round the financial octopus very fast if you are untrustworthy, incompetent or given to long term predictions of your company's performance that ignore reality.

You should use judicious entertaining of your merchant bankers, your brokers, your City solicitors, the heads of finance houses, the financial managers of the insurance companies and pension funds to convince them that you are sober, still young enough to be conscious, have restrained personal tastes, are an adequately conformist dresser, and are competent, gentlemanly, thoughtful, patient and quite capable of reading the Sunday lesson in your local church.

If I make it all sound a bit like a homily from *Scouting for Boys*, that is, I am afraid, rather what it has to be.

## DWARFS, GEOGRAPHIC

The complexes of human beings are myriad, usually untreatable once established and often based on slight variations from the fashionable ideal of birth, stature or skin colour. Everyone knows that small men may have a Napoleon complex. Fewer remember funny little family influences like the observation that the oldest child is likely to be a melancholic, resentful and secretive, whereas the second one may be noisy, assertive, bossy and violent.

Another example that perhaps needs more study is the effect on men from some small nations when they come to work in corporations in bigger countries like the United States. Norwegians, Danes, Belgians and Dutchmen are mostly nice, capable people; but there is the odd one who is mal-adjusted anyway, and some-

where imprisoned in his subconscious may be the fatal
flaw of knowing that the country that nurtured him is
of no account on the world stage and may even have a
risible culture or language. He will compensate like
mad with energy, confidence and aggression; but, just
as a small man's impotent size will leave a nerve somewhere permanently raw, so you may find that a Dutch-
man, for instance, will suddenly show the stigmata of
Geographic Dwarfism under stress. In a multinational
modern corporation these symptoms may be lethal to
someone eventually.

You probably think I am joking; but I once knew a
top executive who had been born in Nicaragua. It was
a dangerous piece of information just to know this,
let alone ever to mention it.


## *DRINK*

I know an executive of outstanding ability who spends
his afternoons in limbo, asleep at his desk, because he
always gets pie-eyed at lunchtime. His company tried
twice to fire him, but he had a contract, and out-
manoeuvred them. He is still there, slurred of speech
and embarrassing to everyone; and I honestly doubt
whether he has ever admitted to himself that he spends
half his working day completely pissed.

It was with cases of self-delusion like this in mind
that Alcoholics Anonymous devised a twenty question
self-test so that people could assess their degree of
alcoholism. Anyone who answers 'yes' to three of the
questions given below is most likely to be an alcoholic,
and answering 'yes' to even one is already an indication that you may have a problem. The questions are

C

a bit tautological, but there is no doubt that they will help escapist executives who have mysteriously failed to admit to themselves that their days may be numbered unless they take themselves in hand. The questions are:

(1) Do you lose time from work because of drinking?

(2) Is your home life unhappy because of your drinking?

(3) Do you drink because you are shy with other people?

(4) Is it affecting your reputation?

(5) Have you got into financial difficulties because of drinking?

(6) Do you feel remorse because of drinking?

(7) Do you turn to lower companions and inferior environment when drinking?

(8) Does it cause you to be careless of your family's welfare?

(9) Has your ambition decreased through drinking?

(10) Do you crave a drink at a definite time daily?

(11) Do you want to drink next morning?

(12) Has your efficiency decreased through drinking?

(13) Do you have difficulty in sleeping as a consequence of drinking?

(14) Is it jeopardising your job or business?

(15) Do you drink to escape from worries or troubles?

(16) Do you drink alone?

(17) Have you ever suffered complete loss of memory?

(18) Has a doctor ever treated you for drinking?

(19) Do you drink to build up your self-confidence?

(20) Have you ever had treatment in a hospital for drinking?

It is perhaps a little naïve to ask a question like number 14 and expect to get an honest answer; if a man is deluding himself, one of his principal delusions will be that whatever hideous self-indulgence he is involved in, it is not affecting his job or business. But the purpose of the litany of questions is to try and make people think, by sheer repetition, what they are doing to themselves.

Incidentally some of the questions, notably number 7, will apply equally tellingly to the other self-destructive habituation, women.

## *DEATH WISH*

In the old days when I was even more intolerant than I am now, I worked for a time under a man who had asked me so many uncomfortable questions, both in notes and at meetings, and made me do so much unnecessary work or repeat so many tasks that were a waste of time in the first place, that I only needed to see his sloping handwriting on the outside of an envelope brought into my office to jump to my feet and shout 'And what does that nit-picking bullying oaf want me to waste my time on now?' Although he probably thought that he had got me successfully and productively on the run in man-management terms, he had actually so wildly overdone the goading that, if I was a violent man, I would long ago have clamped my fingers round his windpipe.

I remember the first time when I realised fleetingly

that he might be human, perhaps even lovable to some. He came into my office while I was on the telephone and stood quietly looking at the large map of the world that was on the wall. When I finished, putting a thin, questing finger at a spot on the map, he said expressionlessly, 'When I retire, that is where I will go.' Seething with my then usual mixture of anger and fear, I walked with difficulty across to look. His finger rested in the sea off Malaysia opposite a tiny green atoll marked 'Phuket Island'.

You will understand that I had allowed myself to fall into a pattern of enraged reflexes at any contact with the man that were just as unreasoning as those that enabled me earlier to ride a bicycle, but far less useful; and much more dangerous. I intended to leave that company at the first opportunity anyway, but if I had stayed I know I would have collected round me a group of malcontents (in another company such a disaffected executive was known as the Escape Officer because he spent most of his business time finding colleagues other jobs). Who knows, perhaps I was simply being my own worst enemy, over-reacting to a relatively straightforward situation, and failing to realise that the man who seemed to persecute me for at least eight hours each day actually only wanted to be friendly.

Just as a lot of people drive to their limit, not because they are in any particular hurry but because they feel competitive with other motorists and they need the excitement, so many executives like me tour round the offices like unexploded bombs just waiting for a small criticism or order from above to detonate them. In the long run it can become wearisome to your chairman or managing director to see you when face to face always fighting with yourself not to be forcefully rude to him; and he may discover that you take every opportunity to tell even perfect strangers what a tool of management he is, and how sadly he abuses you, because one of your unwilling auditors will probably turn out to be a neighbour, cousin, or executive in a friendly company. In the book *Games People Play* the author refers to people who are walking accidents waiting to happen, but he does not suggest how they can get rid of the need. I can only say that, if you are one of us, and you feel an attack of Death Wish coming on, lock yourself in a handy lavatory and read the sombre chapter on what you have to lose.

## *DREAM MERCHANTS, MANAGEMENT*

When I first reached the status a few years ago, I bought a book by a distinguished author called *The Role of the Managing Director*. On the front page it said: 'The position of the managing director is essentially a precarious one.' This statement, daily demonstrated as true, filled me with unease and I never read any further. But the book sat on my shelf as concrete evidence that I had taken my elevation seriously.

I suspect that the same is true of the elegant, penetrating, joky and astute works of the Management Dream Merchants which I see ornamenting the shelves of executives everywhere. They are part of a visible demonstration of the desire by the man concerned to be up-to-the-minute on mid-Atlantic management thought. But do they ever really read them? Or, if they do, how much practical help are they? A writer in a Sunday newspaper mentioned the other day that he had seen a pile of these trendy books heaped on a business friend's shelves, so he asked him for one single valid principle that he had read in all that coherent, astute verbiage and subsequently put into practice. The businessman could not think of one.

I believe that the books about the business ethos which have had really wide readership, and subsequently been well-remembered, are the iconoclastic ones or the ones that look past the exterior labels on men into the beast that slumbers underneath, such as Townsend's *Up the Organisation*, Lorenz's *On Aggression*, Morris's *The Naked Ape* and *Human Zoo*, *The Peter Principle* and, oldest and most time-honoured of all, *Parkinson's Law*. Do not think for a moment that I am condemning the admirable books (and films) produced by current high priests of new techniques. What I am saying is that if you are endeavouring to screw your performance up to a state where it is unimpeachable by the most bloody-minded assassin, then I recommend you to do so by:

(1) Getting factual information out of textbooks on accounting, tax law, advertising or sales force control, rather than subjective information presented by masters of entertaining theory.

(2) Realising that it is impossible to have too much knowledge of animal behaviour to ensure your survival. If you study yourself during an average day, you will find that you take offence at least half a dozen times—at your wife, because she reproaches you for not throwing enough away; at another driver because he makes a two-fingered sign at you after you have sounded your horn at some ill-judged manoeuvre of his;

at your factory manager because he contradicts you in a way that makes you feel ridiculous; at your secretary because she tells you sharply at five o'clock that she has an unbreakable date when you wanted her to take some vital minutes far into the night (all those bottles of perfume, all those half days off, all that charisma from you; wasted).

If that is how you feel, so does your boss. Men are essentially irritable, aggressive, murderous animals, and a knowledge of what turns these reflexes on is the really vital one for survival. Wall Street and the Dow Jones index are crashing through the floor. So do you think that your American President will be looking for your visionary ideas on marketing? Not a bit of it. He will be looking for a scapegoat, a corporate nuisance who can be publicly executed to placate the bizarre gods that preside over share prices.

*EXPENSES*

In a company that I knew once the chief financial
executive also had, year by year, the vastest expendi-
ture on his expenses account. He had a prodigious
thirst, two wives and half a dozen assorted children,
as well as a weakness for a bit of spare and subsidised
good suits. You might well think that in his position he
would be one of the few that could get away with it.
But they got him in the end when, as the mythology
of the case had it, his intercontinental carousals began
to cost the company over twenty thousand pounds a
year. The fact that he was also good at his job did not
save him.

To most young executives, the sudden right to spend
almost limitless sums of someone else's money produces
an acquisitiveness comparable only with the devotion
to duty that a new ram shows when led into a sheep

pen. I remember once seeing a young executive on his first business trip, passing through the duty free shop at Orly airport. A bottle of port in one pocket, cognac in another, an expensive alarm clock ticking in his hand, a plastic bag of assorted perfumes hanging from his wrist, his eye was feverishly bright with cupidity as he darted from shop to shop. Taxi fares and sundry drinks to the value of at least thirty pounds were duly invented by him to cover it all. A lot of you may get away with versions of this for ever—even a managing director will hesitate to provoke the ecstasy of injured innocence that any challenge of an expense account brings on; but the fact remains that most of us, on a large scale or a small one, are robbing our companies. Sometimes it is plausibly accidental; often we excuse ourselves by saying 'Well, I'm always spending my own money for the bloody company anyway and forgetting to put it down.' I am not concerned with the morality of it on this occasion, but merely with reminding you that fiddling your expenses is unlikely to be the principal reason why you are suddenly shot down. But if you are one of those numerous executives whose debits have a permanent question mark over their veracity, it just won't help when your new product launch sinks into the peaty water without a ripple; when it becomes clear that your negligence has ensured that the new project started by the company has a fatal flaw; or when a blunder into a collision with the Inland Revenue authorities obviously stems from you. As your chief executive, I would say to myself, 'That chap is so busy looking after No. 1 and fiddling his expenses, he has no time to think about me and the company'. And I would tell the company psychologist to get out his bloodless annihilator.

## *ENTREPRENEURS*

There are tensions in these people (I nearly wrote us, but modesty spasmed me) that defy analysis. I would have said that they reached out into their environment with a nakedly male aggressivity, then I remembered all the raving queers and fluffy little pinky blonde girls I know who blast off successful businesses and careers. Obviously they have all or most of the following: energy, charisma, style, drive, organising ability, imagination, discipline, perfectionism, maniacal attention to detail, ESP, foresight, courage, gambling ability, and single-mindedness. But one thing a lot of you have in common is a dislike of routine administration. You enjoy the surging adrenalin of the take off, but not the levelling off for straight flight. In fact it turns you off and bores you. I know that you can point to obsessional individuals like Charlie Blühdorn, who started with a few bob like many others and is still there at the top as the now mastodon-like Gulf & Western Corporation that he founded nears the two thousand million dollar turnover mark. But the plain fact is that success softens most men (or women); it can bore them and as a consequence they begin to pore less over the telemetric data from the engine room. If you are an employee who started something from scratch there is probably an even chance that your growing insouciance will cost you your job.

So really you can do one of two things; take Robert Townsend's advice and pack in your job every five years in favour of doing something totally new and different. Or take the risk of staying on and hoping that your sluggish metabolism will keep enough tension in it for you to retain a semblance of vivacity. The latter is much more likely if it is your own money that you are playing with, hence the extreme desirability of getting a share of the equity if you are an employee managing director.

By and large entrepreneurs are rare and wayward creatures; their natural enemies are the second generation organisation men who are normally brought in to tidy the place up when the launch pad has been left well below. An entrepreneur hates an organisation man because of the pedestrian stability of the latter; because his energy may only be available in modest volumes, but always predictably; because the OM's imagination leaves off where the entrepreneur's begins; because an OM is better off without charm, whereas the entrepreneur even if he hasn't charm will be followed by people in droves just out of curiosity; because the entrepreneur does his thing with what appears to be honesty but is in fact an inability to do otherwise, whereas the OM does the boss's thing because he is a good servant, not a master. OMs will try to touch the hem of your gown until the moment when something or someone has extracted the virtue out of you. Then, quite suddenly, they will become cannibals. Entrepreneurphages.

## FOREIGN TRAVEL

A few years ago now I started a scientific study called Pegasus in collaboration with TWA. We flew eight women and six men to California and back over a period of twenty-eight days, checking their blood and urine every four hours, and their judgement, reasoning power, reactions, mood and many other physical and mental parameters once daily. Four men had their sleep constantly monitored. The purpose of the study was to try to get to the bottom of the malaise known as 'jet lag' or 'time zone disease' which catches nearly everyone who suffers a time zone change longer than six hours in a modern jet plane. The subject, at a time when many executives are judged partly by the number of thousands of jet miles that they put behind them in any one year, is obviously of great importance. The study indicated that the stresses are severe enough to make most girls tearful under the slightest strain for at least a day after a non-stop flight from California, to cause sleep and digestive disturbances in both sexes for up to a week, to affect hormone production, to make judgement falter and reaction times double, and generally to make the subject unstable and inefficient. Regrettably, the study became a political hot potato in my then corporation because of the amount of attention that it attracted from radio and television, and hence Wall Street, so that it finally ground to a halt.

Obviously if the results had become available properly, all the subjective observations that men and women have made over the years could have been codified, and management and executives would have been clearly aware of the amount of harm that is being done, voluntarily and involuntarily, to the minds and frames of the wretched executives involved. There are companies in which the chairman makes policy statements like 'Overseas we must fertilise the markets with our feet', and as a consequence his men are hounded across the time zones on constant journeys which are frequently fruitless and sometimes actually counter-productive. A London coroner in the summer of 1971 commented acidly on the travel schedule of an executive who was found dead after travelling continuously on jet planes for nearly two days and two nights.

I am not saying that travel of the Lord Stokes variety is anything but praiseworthy; but I do believe that in many companies, the assumption that marketing and technical managers will spend long periods away from their homes and desks on symbolic hunting trips is not only arrogant. It is a means of ensuring the subjection of the men and women involved. Of making certain that they will not be at the office to plot and cause trouble, and that each time they come back with the fruits or disasters of their journey to be judged anew. It is much easier to point to a hash made of local negotiations carefully reported on than it is to diffuse correspondence lasting years that went wrong somewhere indefinable.

Resist if you can the steely-eyed chairman or general manager who gazes with scorn at you and says: 'So what's stopping you from hopping on a jet plane and going to Venezuela tonight?' Everything is, including your desire to avoid being converted by your early forties into an alcoholic, heavy-smoking, over-travelled extinct volcano.

## GRINDING DOWN

In every company there is at least one executive who is being Ground Down. I just hope that it isn't you. But whoever it is, the boot heel is being rotated down for one of the following reasons:

(1) The political head of a major section has been amputated, and his successor, who was almost certainly one of the assassins, is in process of flushing out all the henchmen left in the wainscoting. This is a process rather like the losses of office that go on in America when a President has gone and all his political appointments automatically come up for review. It is tempting to say that you can do one of two things if you are politically tainted. The first is to try desperately to emulate the chameleon. And the second

is to fling yourself into support of the group that may ultimately dethrone the new boss. Prayer is statistically useless in these circumstances. There are a lot of American companies in this regrettable state. It seems to be a function of progress.

(2) You have become ailing, pathetically old (i.e. over fifty) or failed to grow with the company because of genuine incapacity. Here the best you can hope for is a painless early retirement. And if you have sensibly been Moonlighting (q.v.) it is *much better* to do this than to become really ill in the baneful presence of a boss who is trying to push you out.

(3) There is a sort of senior executive who feels obligated to put the goad in most mornings without realising just how upsetting it can be to subordinates who are conscientious and who may already be overworked. Furthermore, if the top man has an inadequate sense of priorities due to insufficient contact with the business (which is very likely) he may have his men dashing about on useless tasks, neglecting things that they know to be important. This is the most ghastly form of Grinding Down because it is not their fault, but they could well ultimately be fired for incompetence. Here is an invitation to do a bit of assassinating of one's own in sheer self-preservation.

(4) Lack of empathy. Some directors are unable to separate their emotions from their business judgement. They do not like you, so they lean on you. If their dislike is based on something readily remediable, such as your failure to use

deodorants, to discard your ancient and grubby moleskin waistcoat or to try to moderate your Brummy accent when the board are all plummily Oxbridge, then you can do something about it. But if it is basic animal antagonism, you will just be making trouble for yourself by sticking around to be stood on. But you might as well choose a moment of maximum inconvenience to pull out, so that the director concerned is not tempted to repeat his injustice.

(5) If you are able, fast-moving, virile, adequately good-looking and not afraid to show your confidence in yourself, you will make enemies all the way up the tree until you are chairman or managing director. They will not all be jealous contemporaries; some will be threatened older men. Remember that Robert Ardrey said that among swordtail fish being frozen slowly in their tank, the last instinct that they showed as freezing point approached was status consciousness—stronger even than sex. So if that status is threatened, the reaction is murderous. Make sure then that your boss is Jim Slater before you make it obvious how remarkably bright you arc. Otherwise you may find yourself beneath a vengeful boot heel.

D

## HANDSHAKE
### (*Golden or Base Metal*)

Let us assume for a moment that the well-meaning assistance of this book has been proffered in vain, and you have been summoned to an interview which you know is the beginning of the handshake procedure. You are as well-armed as anyone facing execution can be because you know that:

(1) You have some alternative sources of money available to you (see *Moonlighting*).

(2) You are going to drive a very hard bargain over your handshake—remember at an early stage to say that you wish to consult your lawyers before proceeding; contend that your company car is not given to you to perform your work in, but is part of your remuneration; demand that your

pension be continued until you are accepted into an alternative scheme or you retire, which-ever is the longer; and say flippantly that your article for the *Sunday Times* Business News on 'The Rise and Decline of a Great Company' (his) only requires the finishing touches.

(3) Remember you now have nothing whatever to lose and that there are certain general rules about these interviews:

    (a) Your boss does not want to have a prolonged ugly scene, or to be made to feel that he is losing control of the discussion.

    (b) He does not want adverse publicity for his company or himself.

    (c) Most men dislike the accusation of being miserly.

    (d) Many bosses prefer to give away things (cars, furniture, tape-recorders, etc.) rather than money because it looks better in the accounts, so offer to accept tangible alter-natives to money—you can enjoy flogging them later.

Remember that it will take you a year to match your present salary if you are earning over five thous-and pounds a year, so that you cannot accept less than a year's salary. You have probably over the aeons of your employment become accustomed to showing a certain servility towards your boss—perhaps even calling him 'Sir'; now is the time to lose it. You are just two mature males meeting in single combat for which the outcome is going to be fatal for you per-sonally. In zoological terms, you must withdraw from him every advantage that he has. So call him

'Dagleish' as if he were your fag at public school because if you call him 'Sir' or Mr Dagleish you will be psychologically conditioned to accept his terms rather than lay down your own.

If you are a senior person, as I assume, he is probably trying to get you to say that you will resign. So say resolutely and at an early stage that you will resign from his company only if he gives you at least two years' salary, a car, your pension, and your office tape-recorder. And that if he doesn't he will have to carry you physically into the street, while you kick and struggle. He will be nonplussed by this alternative.

I am assuming two things of course. The first is that there is no question of making an action stick for Wrongful Dismissal. You have to remember that any company owner has the right to rid himself of anyone in his company provided that he respects the requirements for notice—in your case probably at least three months. And secondly, I am supposing that you have no contract. If you do have one, then of course you will make the company perform it to the letter.

Why do I stop at a miserable two years' salary? Only because nowadays handshakes of over five thousand pounds are taxable at the ordinary rate, which means that you may have heartbreaking experiences at the hands of the Inland Revenue, without much advantage for yourself, if you go for a thirty thousand pound handshake. Unless of course you know a fabulous accountant.

Ten thousand pounds is a useful sum, however, even after being reduced by tax and the cost of living while you are looking for a good job; it is one of the few ways in Modern Britain of acquiring a substantial nest-egg of capital. Two or three well-judged golden handshakes in your thirties and you're made.

Remember that the British Army learned hundreds of years ago that the parade ground was the secret of steadiness under fire. The guardsman who had been through a sequence of movements thousands of times in safety was programmed to do them with cool courage when shells were bursting all around. So rehearse your terminal interview from time to time, and in moments of real peril keep a regularly revised list of your demands. A final note: your boss will try to crumble you up by verbally listing the things that you have not done, or done incompetently. It is only worth arguing if there are demonstrable errors in what he says. Otherwise sit impassively through, simply saying 'Have you quite finished?' when he pauses for breath.

I probably make it sound as if I think that all such interviews are hostile. This is not so. I am simply not concerned with really amicable arrangements; but it is clear that every year there is an increasing tendency to shed people in the heartless American fashion, without, however, the concomitant American salaries that make the proceedings less traumatic because you have a fat reserve. *The Michelin Guide* suggests that when you go into a hotel or restaurant, it helps if you are seen to be carrying a recent copy of their excellent publication. I respectfully suggest that you might go into your exit interview carrying a copy of this book.

I remember a friend of mine going for a terminal interview at one of the seedier West End hotels—his hatchet-men had not much sense of style. Saying that he would not conclude the interview until he had seen his lawyers, he left them for three hours, and nonchalantly went downstairs to 'phone some business consultants whose advertisement he had observed weeks before for a managing director. Literally minutes later he was being interviewed for his next job. Such alertness and coolness under fire is what you must cultivate in the homicidal climate of modern international business.

## INCOMPETENCE

I am sorry to say that you are incompetent. How can I be so certain? Because everyone is. It is not just that I believe in the Peter Principle which ordains that everybody is promoted until they reach and pass their Level of Incompetence. It is that, if you give me half an hour of your time, I will find an area of your professional or commercial knowledge which is inadequate to do your job properly. You are an accountant? Do you know all the provisions of the last Finance Act? Have you read the latest company reports of your ten major competitors? What percentage of your debts are more than two months old? What proportion of your total factory workers pay is overtime? Sooner or later I will find a blank area in you. And, if I wanted to, carolling loudly with *Schadenfreude*, I could make this an excuse for firing you, any of you. So remember, no one is safe if an assassin—whether a superior or a subordinate—really decides to go for him. But this is also true of your would-be assassin. So, if you detect the dreaded symptoms of potential homicide in someone in your own entourage (see *Assassins*) you must study their work pattern to find their own area of incompetence so that effective counter-charges can be made. A marketing director who is hunting you, for example, but who himself has a pathological inability to go out with the representatives to face the customers. A technical director whose sense of priorities puts the easy problems first on the list so that the hard ones are never dealt with. A managing director who is incapable of speaking coherently in public. A research director who never produces a practical novelty. Remember that, just as every man has his price, so the most effective bluffer can be shown to be inadequate if you devote the necessary time to analysing him. In this field, above all, attack is the most productive form of defence.

## *INGRATITUDE*

'No man will ever forgive another his charity,' said Molière. It is possible to see constant demonstrations of this; perhaps the most striking in recent history was the attitude of the proud, withdrawn General de Gaulle to Sir Winston Churchill. De Gaulle was an amazing and heroic man, but the fact remains that, without Churchill, France would have been crushed for ever. And de Gaulle could never forgive that.

If giant statesmen can behave thus, it should not surprise you that your executives can. In 1956 I remember passing on the offer of a general manager's job in Belgium that I did not want to a younger executive I knew. As a gesture of gratitude (I suppose) he subsequently invited me out to dinner, but throughout the evening never said why he was doing so. And then I did not hear from him again until ten years later when he needed another job.

Massive and long-lasting gratitude is not a normal human emotion. All managers know that every year when they have reconsidered salaries, three-quarters of those who receive pay rises will look disappointed and say 'Oh, is that all?' or words to that effect, when you tell them that you have put up their salary by ten per cent. Most will not thank you at all, and do not seem to notice the granting of non-contributory pension schemes any more than they would the giving of stock options or profit-sharing ones. A company car below someone's station will be grumbled about, but an excessively good car will usually pass unremarked.

The significance of all this is that you may be naïve enough to think that, in the years you have run your company, you have built up a great fund of loving gratitude for kindnesses and acts of generosity. You will be wrong. If you should have the misfortune to be defeated in the board room, a few executives will shake your hand, some may even say that they have learnt something from you. But you are unlikely ever to experience gratitude that shows itself by springing to your defence. You are on your own, and it could even be, as Molière said, that your kindness will only result in people being the readier to take a kick at you. This is not cynicism; only realistic observation.

## JOB, DOING YOUR

Since you are probably a five thousand pound a year man, I ought to hesitate to lecture you about doing something that you certainly do better than I ever could. But this knowledge does not inhibit the average management consultant, so that I do not propose to let it stop me.

First, a few simple mechanical things. You know all the arguments for bad timekeeping—'I stay late, so that authorises me to arrive late.' 'I give the company weekends and evenings whenever they want them, so they can give me half an hour every morning.' But in fact bad timekeeping is merely a concomitant of other increasing tendencies to give less value for money —grog or women in business hours, or an escapist desire to wander round the shops when you should be reading your pending tray. If you can possibly force yourself to keep better time, you will be very grateful when in due course the bushes rustle all round you with assassins looking for a quantifiable series of black marks against you.

Second, remember what Bagehot said in 1870: 'The path to political preferment lies through orthodoxy.' This is still true in business, as elsewhere. Chairmen, boards of directors, the City, ministers and kings may all protest loudly that what they want is unorthodox corner-cutting, but actually, with very few exceptions, they do not. Biology proceeds down the millenia with almost imperceptible advances, always ready to scuttle back into the safety and anonymity of the previous evolutionary step if things go wrong and a dinosaur results. This is exactly how most corporations are. Giant strides or sudden changes of direction produce a fundamental feeling of insecurity in nearly everyone involved, and the executive concerned will in due time come to be regarded as a dangerous threatener of the commercial ecology. Sooner or later the representatives of the status quo will gang up on him. So only innovate sparingly and when you are forced to do so.

Similarly, if you are concerned—as you should be—with getting the best out of your company, remember when you are tempted to reorganise what Gajus Petronius wrote in AD 66:

We trained hard, but it seemed that every time we were beginning to form up into teams, we would be reorganised. I was to learn later in life that we tend to meet any new situation by reorganising, and a wonderful method it can be for creating the illusion of progress, while producing confusion, inefficiency and demoralisation.

Nothing much has changed in the intervening nineteen hundred years.

Resist the call to be a Guerilla Fighter in business hours. In big companies the temptation is to throw in your lot with those who spend hours a day in discussing current company politics; some of these men are even prepared to do things that are totally to the company's detriment in order to spite a colleague or gain a political advantage. This kind of irresponsibility is playing into the hands of a determined assassin. If you are discontented, analyse why and do something about it. Bloody easy, you'll say, to go and tell your chairman that you need more money, or that the twenty notes that he writes you a day are driving you up the wall. I know that it isn't easy, but a craven discontent with your lot will rot you much quicker than a short, sharp interview, regardless of the outcome.

Ask yourself whether you have learned any new skills lately. If the answer is that over the last twelvemonth you have not even studied how your invoicing machine works, let alone attended a one day computer taxation or Common Market orientation course, you may have shut your mind to new information, and this can ossify you quite soon, as well as providing a potential assassin with useful evidence of loss of grip.

Everybody in British management must be aware of the activities of Jim Slater and his group—buying companies, ripping out the assets, selling off part of them so that the original purchase price is reduced to nothing, then driving the company forward in pursuit of one goal; increasing profitability. Such penetrating comprehension and single-mindedness is clearly beyond most of us, but the one executive that even the ruthless

Slater organisation would never banish is he who is productively profit-obsessed.

Stop thinking about increasing your sales. Think about making more on each sale. Is your advertising budget wasteful? Yes, they always are. Cut out the prestige advertising, it's too slow burning. Hack down your PR costs. If you are paying more than ten thousand pounds for them then you are probably setting about them the wrong way, anyway. Do not launch products about which you have doubts. Nothing supports a charge of incompetence like a dud launch. Prune your staff; the fewer they are the more purposefully they will work. Get your switchboard girl whenever she is asked for a line, to say: 'Is it a personal call?' Fifty per cent of the staff will lie and say 'No', but you will save a substantial sum on the other fifty per cent. Look hard at the travelling expenses of your subordinates, particularly taxis. It is amazing how many pounds some executives can claim to have spent just in criss-crossing quite small towns.

Put up your prices if you can. I know all about competition, but I have also sold things at much higher prices than almost identical items from other manufacturers just by relying on the widespread belief that something more expensive is better—the state of mind that made a famous nineteenth-century wife say: 'We are too poor to be able to buy cheap things.' Remember that selling half the number of goods at twice the profit margin reduces the distribution, inventory and invoicing costs.

Finally, remember that if you are so overworked that you cannot do your job properly any more, something is really wrong. It may be any of the following:

(1) You like being overworked because you have a guilt complex, or because it enables you to say: 'I can't do my job properly because I am too overworked'.

(2) You are an extremely inefficient worker, writing things by hand when you should dictate them, muddling into detail that belongs to your subordinates, or reading the *Financial Times* when you should be doing something important.

(3) You are genuinely overworked and need more assistance, but are too insecure to demand it.

(4) You have subordinates to whom you refuse to delegate because you cannot accept that three times as much work done half as efficiently is still better than your own performance.

(5) You are so incapable of doing your job that your getting fired will be the best solution, because otherwise you will kill yourself running to try vainly to keep up.

## KING-MAKING

It is said that the Chinese, when studying the psychology of escape during the Korean war, found that if they observed the prisoners closely for a few days they could weed out all the leaders. They were not necessarily all officers—some indeed were privates. But once these were safely segregated in special security camps, the remaining ninety-eight per cent of prisoners never tried to escape and gave no trouble.

In spite of desperate attempts by management consultants, the Government, unions, training boards, technical colleges and others, no satisfactory means has emerged of increasing the output of real leaders above the biologically-ordained two per cent. This is the most unpalatable fact for socialists, and is the ultimate reason why all animals will never be equal.

My purpose in mentioning this beastly fact here is

not to provoke political polemics, but to say that it is quite easy for an executive who feels himself vulnerable to identify a genuine leader in his company environment. It will be someone—he may even be junior to the threatened executive—who seems to know what he is doing; is stable and non-moody; generally does a task more thoroughly than is really required so that he always has something in reserve; has the self-criticism that a sense of humour brings; makes sensible, unostentatious but frequent contributions at meetings; and has that indefinable charisma that makes people want to follow him in good situations and bad. Perhaps the man sounds ripe for election to Chief Scout; and of course not every business has the luck to have a young man with such an obvious future. All I am saying is that if you should find one around during some tough sledding and you can have the courage to admit that, however worthy you are, he has a greater future, back him. If he is that regular, he will not forget your support in the years to come. Remember that overestimating your own ability is a killing disease. And making a sober assessment that you have found a young oak which can one day shelter you is not just modesty; it is the foresight that can save your life when the lightning is about.

## LOSE, WHAT YOU MAY, IF ASSASSINATED

A highly qualified doctor, who was also a senior executive in industry, was once suddenly assassinated by his company. Years afterwards he told me that the experience had damaged some mechanism in him which he believed now might never recover. Other victims have told me that the main casualties in their personalities were their self-confidence, creativity and aggressivity.

If one studies male pack leaders in animal behaviour (and managing directors are only this) then one sees that, immediately they are defeated by a younger or stronger adversary, their morale collapses and they will often die prematurely from going into a sort of decline. This in turn is because, in physiological terms, success breeds success. A man who is charging forward unstoppably produces correspondingly more male

E

hormones which to an extent are both at the base of a robust male physique and an aggressive reaching out into his potentially hostile surroundings. In turn, male success is integral in natural selection and in deciding who has the right to breed. It is no accident that the strongest single attractant to the human female is power (usually allied to money, which is often the same thing). And obviously a male who has failed spectacularly once can expect to be eliminated by the same ruthless natural system.

So the worst loss of the assassination victim is likely to be his own potency, in every sense of the word. This may be so bad that it amounts to a virtual death sentence in a few cases. In a few others, recovery may seem to be complete although the lesson will almost certainly never be forgotten. The great mass of victims are in the middle; deeply hurt, temporarily paranoid, bewildered, bitter, most of these symptoms will disappear if and when they are again in comparable employment. But it can be a big 'if' for those many men who are one to two stone overweight, bald and generally look ten years older than their fortyish years.

Next, it goes without saying that the women in his life will probably abruptly ask themselves what they are doing dragging around with this burnt-out hulk. Not your wife; if you are lucky she has already stuck with you for ten to twenty years, and had few illusions anyway. I am thinking of your bits of side business, who may have been very important to you, but who will now feel the biological call to go to the highest bidder.

If you are a director, your car goes. If it cost the company three thousand pounds, then you are going to have to find six thousand pounds in pre-tax money to replace it identically; or else you will have to explain to the local community why you have suddenly dropped out of the Jaguar class. You may lose a chauffeur, an inestimable asset in parking-meter-ridden towns, and when an otherwise long commute needs to be made profitable.

You will lose your pension, and the older man may find it difficult and expensive to get an adequate replacement. You will lose access to the company flat in town, and the company yacht if it was that sort of self-indulgent organisation. Your children's school fees may cease to be paid from a Bahamian account. The people you hired at your old company will suddenly be embarrassed to meet you, in case you go into paeans of self-pity or wild accusations of those who survived or replaced you. And you will learn for the first hideous time to wait in line with patient Pakistanis and pot-smoking hippies at the Labour Exchange while official manoeuvres take place with your National Insurance card.

The soapbox from which you fulminated on television at the last budget has been kicked away from underneath you, because as you are no longer the managing director of the Surplice-Makers Company, you have neither position nor size. In fact overnight you are no one and have reverted to the ranks of the New Poor.

I expect you can find gaps in this doom-laden list, such as denial to you of an incredibly favourable staff shop, or loss of a gardener-handyman who was offici-ally your factory storeman. My point in drawing up this liturgy is not to be exhaustive, but just to show you that your losses will be incalculable if you do not Look Behind You really effectively *now*.

## MOONLIGHTING

Every day as a managing director you use a wide spread of skills—you talk fluently, criticise penetratingly, persuade, sell, negotiate, speak foreign languages, analyse contracts, charm socially, write lucid prose and show many other aptitudes. Some or all of these are equally true if you are the marketing, production, research, technical or any other director, and you may have specific professional skills besides. In competitive modern business, so much may be demanded of you that you feel you have no time for anything else. You put yourself in a prison cell of your own construction, and this, quite frankly, is what the company wants. A neat package of a full-time company man over whom their dominion is absolute, and who will go quietly when the time comes.

So analyse your skills for saleable ones and when you come home in the evenings do not just sink slippered into your armchair clutching a whisky as if it would dissolve all your problems. Think of the business that you might set up to liberate yourself. Consider the authoritative series of articles or book that you might write, the photographs you can sell, the translations that you could take in. The outside directorships that you might solicit. The jewellery you could design. The boutique you could help your wife to set up. The real property deals that you could start in a small but growing way. The flowers and fruit you could grow for sale in your garden. There are two advantages to this. The first is that when the worst happens you do not suddenly feel stripped of your total earning power—a terrible feeling. And second, you have something sensible and productive to occupy you at such a time. You may have heard of the directors who, when suddenly fired, continued to take the 8.20 to the City every day and mooched about there until the evening because they simply could not conceive any other daily routine, and had nothing else to turn to.

I am not suggesting that you rob your company of time, or clog the switchboard with private business calls. I am saying that your working day is only eight hours, and you are awake for sixteen in all. If you can rid yourself of the compulsive loyalty that makes you able to think only of one master, you have plenty of time for a subsidiary career that will provide a safety net, add to your earnings, enrich your experience, and keep you amused after the guillotine falls at sixty-five.

## NEEDLESS BRUTALITY

Nowadays overt social paranoia is so commonplace in organisations such as the London School of Economics, and in situations like Ulster and most Trafalgar Square demonstrations, that it would be surprising if it was not frequently found in business as well. Paranoia is part of the psychotic syndrome of schizophrenia, which for the sake of completeness we have to divide into two types: paranoid schizophrenia, usually developing in men between forty-five and fifty-five; and dementia praecox, the psychosis that develops in young people between fifteen and twenty-five. The latter is marked by confusion, withdrawal, and, most terrifying by far, a separation between acts and feelings, so that, for example, competent murders can be carried out by young men without feeling any remorse or disgust.

Seen in this light, it is tempting to think that members of urban guerilla gangs are bonded together by dementia praecox rather than patriotism.

The middle-aged man who develops paranoid schizophrenia is suffering from a chronic, slowly progressive mental disorder, characterised by the development of ambitions or suspicions into systematised delusions of persecution and grandeur which are built up in logical form. The archetype of this sad diagnosis is the mental hospital inmate who believes he is Napoleon, and who thinks that 'they' are plotting against him.

The reason I mention these psychoses is because although only mercifully few relinquish control completely of the savage instincts that live in all of us, nevertheless most people can under stress show paranoid schizophrenic, manic depressive or other symptoms and signs which stop only just short of the deranged. So that it is possible to have a superior who will barely even record that he is bringing you close to suicide with his heartless goading and his burdening of you with his own compulsive attention to senseless detail. This applies also to firing. I knew a man once who boasted that he had fired dozens of executives. I watched him in action once, and it was depressingly obvious that he was actually enjoying getting rid of quite a decent middle-aged chap. A mixed racial background, patchily successful business career, unpleasant marriage and deteriorating health had made him need to lash out at others to make them as miserable as he was himself.

So what can we do about it? You can hardly go in and say to your boss 'I have diagnosed you as a paranoid schizophrenic with manic depressive tendencies.

We are all agreed that people would notice it less if you stopped thinking we are all plotting against you.' He would probably prefer to think that yours was the sick ego. But you can provoke him to make a scene in the presence of someone who is able to do something about it—the shareholders if it is the chairman, or the chairman if it is your managing director. Identify the areas which are triggers for a really senseless rage— like the senior Labour politician who is said to foam at the mention of the BBC—and steer the discussion round to the subject during an executive meeting. Trump up incidents in which the *bête noire* figures, whether it is a person or an organisation, and wave the name and its misdeeds at the manager concerned as a matador would his cape. The idea is to get him charging until his behaviour becomes wild enough for the people who can make changes to bring one about. Besides, it will give you a little satisfaction in your misery to see the other's face empurple and his hands begin to tremble as you set him off.

I speak from real experience here. Once I had a boss appointed over me with such a lack of a sense of priorities and such mad attention to aimless detail that life under him was purgatory. Then, in the spastic manner of that particular company, a brash and much younger vice-chairman was put in over him. Straight-away it was clear that the new man had induced acute paranoia in the older man, so I used to hang around in the car park and upstairs corridor to exchange a few words with the young vice-chairman, then go down to my man and say: 'Just had a word with Mr Chapple. He was asking when you were going to find the Indian contract.'

'Bugger Mr Chapple,' would be the thick-voiced

reply. 'Let him sodding well mind his own bloody business,' and for the next hour he would be incapable of leaning on me, being too busy reflecting on bloodless ways of dismembering the unsuspecting Chapple.

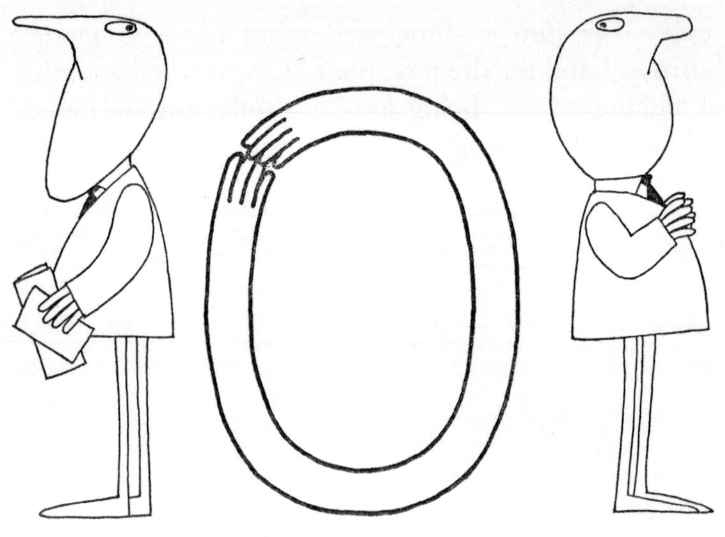

## ODOURS, GOOD AND BAD

When a Frenchman says 'Je ne peux pas le sentir,' he is saying 'I can't bear the man's smell,' although what he means is that he cannot stand the fellow. The German says 'Ich kann ihn nicht riechen,' and the double meaning is exactly the same. There is no doubt that people broadcast from themselves a positive orchestration of scent information, some of it consciously perceptible but much of it apparently absorbed by others without detectable analysis. Little work has been done scientifically on these fascinating elements called pheromones, which undoubtedly have an enormous effect on all human relations including irresistible sexual attractions.

Although if we are rude enough (by which I mean honest enough) to analyse the information that comes to us through our nose from a man that we detest, we

can probably smell stale tobacco, sweat, his after-shave
lotion, the flat, fatty odour of his hair and, if we are
really dealing with a case of neglect, his infrequently
washed socks. But, if he is one of those people who are
widely disliked, sometimes at a distance and on little
or no acquaintance, he must be giving out a more
sinister exhalation than any of these.

I have known two executives who prospered in
office mainly because they were very hard workers,
knowledgeable, intelligent and would do anything
that they were told to do. Both of them were univer-
sally disliked, and I seriously doubt if either had a real
friend anywhere among their vast acquaintanceship.
Both involved themselves in enormous social rounds of
the stereotyped Rotarian variety, and they would
apply themselves with mad devotion to dull and unimportant tasks such as the secretaryship of some
worthy but tinpot society.

Both these men went through their respective companies sowing disorder and generating assassinations
all round them. First, because people who worked for
them came to loathe them so rapidly and completely
that office in their department was tantamount to an
early death sentence. Second, because, feeling the dislike around them all the time, both men would always
tend to be involved in any majority political action
in order not to add to their difficulties by being seen
to defend an unpopular cause. And third, another
characteristic of such men is a certain feminine mallea-
bility, a tendency to mould their opinions to those of
the current Master so that any dissentient would
always tend to find them vocal on the other side.

I expect by now you have recognised the sort of inadequate person I mean—buying his female company

on business trips, normally married to a mouse, completely lacking the streak of attractive madness that Zorba the Greek said quite rightly a man must have to set him free. All I wanted to say here was, if you find that you are working for this type of basically impotent specimen, make other arrangements as quickly as you can if you are an individual of rugged opinions because, sooner or later, he will probably have the humane killer used on you as a polluter of the trouble-free ambience that he must have. And even if he is not your boss, but just a cog in the machine that you yourself control, watch him. In any majority plot against you he will be holding the coat of your major adversary.

## PSYCHOLOGISTS

In the film *The Devils* there was a depraved exorcist who tortured, burned and fornicated, all in the interests of ridding citizens of the evil spirits that had seized them. The passion with which he carried out his functions reminded me, unkindly enough, of the tame psychologists used by American corporations as the executioners of managers who are spent volcanoes or who have become intolerably lubricious or semi-permanently intoxicated. These hired assassins will sidle up to their victims whilst murmuring homicidally that what is about to happen is really in the patient's best interests and has to be done anyway for simple reasons of company hygiene. And sooner or later the victim suddenly stiffens to the prick of the needle that transports him into oblivion.

I do not belong to the group of resolute individualists who quote the fact that sixty per cent of psychiatrists and psychologists admit that they first got interested in the tortured human mind because of concern over their own complexes. There are a lot of lovely psychologists around, I am sure; but you have to remember that, in a company, they have only one ultimate justification: to smell out the intellectually maimed individual, whether at his first interview, at the height of his career, or when his powers begin to fail.

I assume that by now you have analysed yourself and know not only whether you are a small or large company man, but also whether you are a manic depressive, alcoholic, satyr or exhibitionist. Whatever it is that you have pin-pointed, resolve that the last person on earth who is going to be able to file away details of your weakness is the company psychologist. When he puts you through the hoops of his sometimes mercifully naïve tests, do all you can to foul him up by answering the opposite to the reply you are instinctively tempted to give.

Am I preaching revolution here, inciting you to damage your company by concealing the truly parlous state of yourself? No. Psychologists normally tend to overlook that the most creative, productive and successful members of the human race are manic depressives, drunks, or obsessed with sex. If an organisation rejects people merely because they do not conform to a traditional pattern of middle-of-the-road bourgeois behaviour, this is wrong. A man should be judged only on what he achieves. If he is a wild man but also an immensely valuable one, it may be necessary to put him into a rather special framework in an organisation in order to avoid frightening the inherently timorous Wall Street or the shareholders, but executing him via an exorcist is an act which may well only ensure the future mediocrity of your organisation, not its prosperity.

## QUEERS

Last year was a good one for the revival of old English Grundyism. Lord Longford had to retire from two Danish exhibitions of sexual intercourse, and Mrs Mary Whitehouse, who for years has been trying to force her tortuous minority view of what is sexually acceptable on the British television audiences, went off to see the Pope brandishing copies of *Oz* schoolkids issue and the *Little Red School Book* like the school sneak going off to tell all to the headmaster.

I happen to believe that, compared with the lethal consequences of religious polemics, both written and spoken pornography can at best produce a sad introspection which in this century has probably not directly contributed to one death. The same cannot be said, for example, of the religious confrontation in Ulster which seems difficult to equate with the Christianity in the name of which most pornography is condemned.

In England there have been estimated to be three quarters of a million male adult homosexuals. It is also accepted that they are active (or passive) in such organisations as the Church, Army, Parliament, and, undoubtedly, the upper reaches of business.

Everybody has to do their own thing in this world, and it is just as difficult to turn a homosexual into one who delights in luscious members of the opposite sex as it is to turn a left-handed person into a right-handed one. I have included a mini-chapter on this still inexplicably controversial subject only because the Longfords and the Whitehouses (and many others) have shown us again, just recently, how many influential or vocal people there are among us who regard any behaviour that does not happen to appeal to them as disgusting, immoral or a suitable subject for restrictive legislation. If, therefore, you happen to have a left-handed thread, you probably do not need me to remind you how effective it will be in any assassin's indictment for him to be able to finish by saying 'And, of course, the bloody man's a poof as well.' In other words, if you think that the widespread talk about the Permissive Society means that you can stop keeping your head down about the nature of your *ménage*, think again.

It is rather comical to reflect that, in the United States, a country as riddled with homosexuality as our own, all company psychologists go to great pains to try to smell out the queer during psychology tests. The law of averages being what it is, there must be a few left-handed threads in the head-shrinking industry. One wonders how successful these thieves are at catching their fellow thieves.

F

## *REPRESENTATIVES*

Most companies are compelled to have what is now fashionably called an interface with the public. In the case of semi-professional organisations such as the Stock Exchange, it will be restricted to seductively-clad guide-hostesses. But companies selling paints, pharmaceuticals, cars, television, insurance and thousands of other things all have what should be designated salesmen, but which British decorum dictates must be called representatives.

The business simply begins and ends with them. If they offend the customers and put them off your products, then your chairman's eloquence, the managing director's iron discipline, the haughty extrapolations of the MBAs in the corporate planning department and the nationwide clamour of your advertising agents

will largely or wholly have been in vain. This is the
stark truth. But because representatives, let's face it,
seem to the top brass a bunch of *peones* at best, it is
almost impossible for a genuine, warm and fruitful
relationship to arise. Top executives tend to treat
the salesmen they want to cosset in the same way as
white liberals deal with coloured people—with a con-
siderable amount of embarrassed (and embarrassing)
gush. Possibly the solution will be to promote a couple
of salesmen to the board, recognising at last their indispensability and the terrifying consequences to the
business of real inefficiency on their part. But my purpose in mentioning the salesman here was simply to
intone one thing. That if your survival and the company's success depend on a steady sales increase and a
good profit record, you must regard your salesmen as
your most important henchmen. Everybody else just
spends money or counts it. They make it.


## *RAPE, SHOUTING*


I am sure that few observers of the political scene will
have forgotten the expulsion of Lord Hall, Chairman
of the Post Office, in 1971, and the way that he des-
cribed his enforced departure as 'a monstrous rape'.
He used the same four-letter word in two other con-
nections (one of them actually the usual one) during
his spirited defence of himself on radio, television and
in the newspapers. He obviously thought he had had
an exceedingly raw deal, and there are two lessons
here for us:

(1) If you are in the public eye to the extent that

Lord Hall was, a threat that you will see the matter thrashed out on television may well daunt any but the most implacable adversary. But the threat should be made well before the emergency. Shouting rape after defloration has actually occurred never mended anyone.

(2) I am sure that Lord Hall knew what he was doing, but his particular choice of words may not be appropriate for most executives, no matter how deeply hurt. Point to your proud record, to the solidarity of the workers behind you and to your grandiose plans for the future, but do not yield to the temptation of railing in an undignified fashion. You may have to find a comparable job, and your new employers may just not fancy someone who has publicly admitted to being violated.

## SELF-ANALYSIS

Why do so many executives get into such untenable positions that only death or firing will release them? With some, of course, it is the grim realisation that they have passed their Level of Incompetence, are likely to be further promoted, and will then reach a veritable stratosphere of incompetence. They set their teeth and hang on grimly until someone above them is not only observant enough to notice their plight, but ruthless enough to do something about it. Then a tragedy occurs. How could the victim concerned have avoided getting into such a situation? The answer is by analysing himself much more honestly at an earlier stage. For example, if you are a man for small companies, you will be terribly unhappy—and possibly very bad —at playing the big corporation game. Some people feel safe and anonymous sitting in the little niches of big companies, exchanging safely inconclusive memos with their colleagues and rambling away at eternal meetings where dangerous issues are left alone. But in such circumstances, the small company amateur will miss the action, the speed, the informality, the family atmosphere of knowing everyone's name. He will be tempted to move too fast, cut corners, tread on toes, speak his mind, drop out of meetings and take decisions which normally belong higher up the hierarchy. Conversely, the big corporation man, with his great need for warm security, will feel horribly exposed by the rapidity of change and personal responsibility of the small company.

It goes without saying that you should decide with equal care what particular line of business, and what particular department in that business, turns you on. If cars are your thing, and you are selling tobacco, your imagination will probably refuse to run at a proper working temperature, and you may even be tempted to read car literature or dream about them in business hours when you should be concentrating on survival. Do not get into a line function where you have to hire, fire and order people about if you are a bespectacled, quietly reflective egghead who gets a nervous tic at the thought of any of those activities. Conversely, if you are a staff man who just wants to be left to pore over charts and statistics, you are not being sensible if you try and force yourself to be a hairy-wristed marketing director. Do not undertake vast intercontinental journeys—or a job which requires them—if you are paranoid, suffer from constant diarrhoea or crippling insomnia under these conditions. Horatio Nelson may have been a seasick admiral, but he had really outstanding compensating qualities which you may just be lacking.

If you are a misogynist, do not get into the company of women executives; and if you are a compulsive seducer, be quite sure that you know what you are doing before you surround yourself with lovely young personal assistants. If you are already floundering in your present job, do not recommend the taking over of another company which could vastly increase your responsibilities.

If you despise City men as some executives do, either master your feelings when forced into their company by some complex financial manoeuvre, or leave it to more chameleon-like members of your company to hold the hands of the merchant bankers.

Sometimes on business administration courses in the United States, participants are requested to write their own obituaries. Try writing yours, looking icily at your career to date, praising only the real qualities and successes, and implacably listing the failures. It may help you to see yourself as your survivors will see you if you do not do something remedial *now*.

## *STRESS*

Thomas Hickman, basing himself on the work of Dr Victor Howard, a behavioural consultant, announced in an article in the *Sunday Times* of 21 November 1971 that 'this is the era of FACT—Frustration, Anxiety, Conflict, and Tension.' Quoting the Office of Health Economics, he said that one working day in ten is lost through certified sickness among the over-forty-fives; to which a doctor, speaking to an industrial society conference, added that more than half of this absentee-ism is caused by psychological illness.

If you come to think of it, the pressures on your managers increase every year like the squeezing of a cheese press tightened night and morning. You have just got to be more profitable because the City will devalue your shares if you are not, and the owner will fire you if you are a private company. Technology bounds past you, someone is always sniffing about to pick up blocks of your shares, the Government is try-ing to force you to move to development areas, your office workers snarl at you every time you raise their salaries because the increase represents only the amount the cost of living has gone up since their last raise. So you get into a state of FACT in which:

$F=Frustration$. Half-civilised as we are (c.f. the recent activities in Bangladesh and Northern Ireland) we have been taught that we should not attack those who offend us. At least, not physically. The aggression that is thus turned inwards becomes frustration, the battle cry of everyone up to the topmost rung of the executive ladder.

$A=Anxiety$. This apparently gets its intensity from fear in the absence of real danger. It is fear of in-adequacy, of failure, of authority, of decision, of losing status, or of what others think.

$C=Conflict$. Frequently the incompatible demands of two bosses, or one boss versus the obvious needs of the business. Or trying to be individual when everyone is howling for conformity. Or challenge versus security. Or the need to seek higher status and security against the fear that they will mean over-promotion. Or demands of home and family against those of the company.

*T = Tension.* This is a manager's constant companion, and it doubtless accounts for the number of top businessmen who get headaches and lassitude on Saturday morning when the daily adrenalin-induced tension suddenly relaxes. The mobilising of the adrenal glands for fight or flight causes the stomach to churn even when empty, puts up your blood pressure, and tunes up the mind to the point where you may well have difficulty in getting to sleep.

FACT, as defined above, can be the potentially lethal enemy within. Dr Howard gave Mr Hickman the following advice on how to defy it:

(1) Know your strengths and limitations and accept yourself as you are.

(2) Hiding an anxiety may make it worse, so get it out in the open.

(3) Don't expect praise from others in this pitiless world. Soundly based self-respect should need no outside prop.

(4) Keep active. Physical movement and change are necessary in drawing off nervous tension.

(5) Focus on today. You can only live one day at a time, but you can worry about whole years at a time.

(6) Do it now. If you take decisions and act upon them this helps to keep tension down.

(7) Don't waste your time on continual self indulgent defence against criticism.

(8) Maintain a list of priorities, and act on it in the order that you soberly believe is correct.

Your aim should be to make it apparent to friends and colleagues that you are not tense. Just turned on.

## SALVAGING PEOPLE

'There are no bad executives, only badly led ones,' a chairman with a fanatical belief in leadership once said to me. I have since realised now right he was. Organisations almost without exception reflect the strengths and weaknesses of the man at the top. Consultants know this better than anybody, but they are also nearly always hired by the chief executive, so that their witch hunts are conducted at the levels that they know are not the fundamental cause of the trouble. You can hardly tell the man who brought you in to commit hari-kiri. So that the people whom companies murder after the consultants have gone are usually the inadequate little replicas of the man who should actually go.

I mention this mainly because first, it would be nice if an occasional chief executive in homicidal mood would ask himself whether there is something serious that he could do to help a man in temporary trouble, and second, in the future more thought is going to have to be given to easing out top executives in companies where they have become a self-perpetuating oligarchy. This is, for example, frequently the case in large American concerns that have gained a reputation as hire and fire organisations. The incompetence of the top men means that they have to be protected by a human square of cannon fodder that can be riddled with the enemy grapeshot when things go wrong.

Perhaps it is excessively idealistic to expect the top man in this hard, competitive world always to care about salvaging people who, because of trouble at home, illness, overwork, or depression, become temporarily incompetent. But if they don't, I have a feeling that one year a hard-eyed Executives' Union will do it for them.

## *TEA-LADIES*

These are an important sub-branch of the chief executive's intelligence system. Make sure you use them if you are defending your top position, and that you cower away from them if you have anything to hide. After all, who else in the company has reason to visit all the executives' offices, morning, afternoon and evening? Who else can say exactly who is still absent from their offices at morning coffee time, slightly drunk in the mid-afternoon, or asleep at any time, sprawled over their interview couches? Perhaps if I give a few hints on what seem to me the chief executive's proper criteria for recruitment and control of the tea-lady, those who have to defend themselves will see why.

The ideal tea-lady should be comfortably middle-aged, not *senex et horrida* like a Cambridge bedmaker, but kind and innocent-eyed. She should be in speech obviously plebeian so that no suspicions are aroused that she is undercover officer class. She must obviously be a silent mover when necessary, and good at simple deduction. And she must give up her information without appearing to realise that she may be shopping someone. After all, a good tea-lady is often harder to replace than a marketing executive, and we do not want her to feel that over the years she has a number of untimely deaths on her conscience, do we? She must herself be beyond being suborned or seduced even by the most desperate older man. And absolutely never absent for illness or any other reason, but capable of varying the time of her tea rounds if anyone needs special surveillance. Her observation must be trained to be such that with one sweeping glance she takes in the crumpled bra under the desk, the pornographic novel under the blotting pad, and the *Evening Standard* racing page in the half-shut desk drawer.

'Hallo, Mrs Peters' (or, better still, Ivy), you say cheerily to her as she comes into your office, 'How are the feet today (or your grandchildren, roses or pet mongrel)?' It is important that she *loves* you because then not only will she give you information without a qualm, but also she will act as your best propagandist around the whole building; telling people who think of you only as the ultimate shit what a *lovely* man you are.

'Is Mr Harvey in today, do you know?' Momentary pause, 'Yes, but he is looking rather tired.' This is tealadyese for disgustingly exhausted by libidinous excesses. 'Was there anyone with him that I would disturb if I sent for him?'

'Only his secretary.' She does not need to embroider

this, having already said anxiously on a previous occasion that she was afraid that Mr Harvey's secretary wasn't getting a proper lunch because they had asked her to make them two coffees which they drank together in his locked office between midday and two.

## UNWHOLESOME PEOPLE

'Everyone can get on with the nice guys,' said a former superior of mine, 'it's the executives who can get on with the sons of bitches that win through in the end.' He should have known in a perverse sort of way, because he was a monumental son of a bitch himself. But the point is a valid one; just as ninety-eight per cent of the human race is ugly, so at least that percentage can become really cross-threaded under suitable circumstances. The importance of this to the would-be executive survivor is to remember that everyone under his command will hate him bitterly at some time, and indeed he is unlikely to be doing his job properly if they don't. But he must at an early stage make sure that he has consciously classified himself either as (a) a highly efficient shit, or (b) a less efficient

nice guy. If he is unwise enough to become an inefficient shit, then he is certainly doomed. Really efficient
nice guys are, as it happens, in danger of extinction in
modern business anyway, so you are probably wasting
your time classifying yourself in this category.

## *VOGUES*

I happen to have worn long sideburns for about ten years, having grown them originally to diminish the then youthful plumpness of my cheeks, and subsequently felt too conservative to mow them off again now that the need has passed. Whenever I take over an organisation, a slow tendency has become apparent in it for the executives and others to become more hirsute on the cheeks. This silly little observation is however very symptomatic. If your employees identify with you in an empathic way, they are more or less bound to adopt those of your idiosyncrasies that are cheap and do not make them look ridiculous—although if you are a free-spending Rolls-Royce driver you will notice some pressure for improvement in the company cars as well. Thus if a chief executive sports a huge wall map or a brass oil lamp on his desk, offices down the line

G

will begin to develop these, just as a school captain can easily start otiose fashions like leaving a button undone or going about with coat collar turned up. The sub-conscious feeling gets around that it is right to do the boss the honour of imitating him.

Of course these vogues spread through the organisation in many other areas than just dress, facial hair and office decoration. If, for example, the chairman runs the company on a high note of managerial hysteria, this will infect everyone from the representatives up. We all know thoroughly nice companies where everyone is friendly and relaxed, and other companies where a grotty, frightened, withdrawn man sits in every office. This comes from the chief executive in both cases, just as bad parties always reflect hosts who have no gifts for social intercourse. I am not suggesting that you do any-thing about it, although you will be intelligent enough to weigh whether it will be in your long term interest to conform when you have realised that the company game is a dangerous and boring one called cricket; that you are expected to imitate a boss who travels cease-lessly, whether necessarily or not, all over the world throughout the year; and that all the successful execu-tives go on endless orgies of jargon and modish com-mercial behaviour called management courses.

## WALL STREET

(see also *City, Keeping the Love of the*)

I know one or two really charming men in Wall Street, and I hope and expect there are actually thousands. But I also know one or two who are virtually gangsters, and who—as John Brooks pointed out in *Once in Golconda*—are obsessed with money-making as blindly as are koala bears with eucalyptus shoots (although far less lovably).

Years of working with and for American companies have shown me that there is really only one rule. Melt into the background. I remember being astonished the first time I went to Madison Avenue. All the executives were wearing suits that might have been tailored by Montague Burton at the end of the war, striped ties that mimicked regimental ones and heavy punched brogues. There were even turn-ups on their trousers. That was only in the mid-sixties. You have to remember that the United States is a tribal society. Everyone upon arriving in the Promised Land from no matter where, must adopt all the paraphernalia of middle-class rightist Americana as soon as possible to avoid offending the vast mass of those already there. If you don't, you risk the minority persecution which is such a characteristic of that particular society.

And so it is in your relations with Wall Street. You can permit yourself the luxury of being Jewish because it would be pretty hypocritical of many modern members of the Street to persecute you for being that. But anything more extravagant—such as being reported in gossip columns as doing something trendy like dancing nude at a St Moritz party, attacking the tax policy of the government of the day, saying something nasty in public about God, motherhood or the Daughters of the American Revolution—that's foreground stuff, and a Wall Street banker somewhere will be telephoning the Death Squad to get you out before your leaps in the limelight affect your company's stock prices.

If you really want Wall Street to love you until you are ready to be deep-frozen for the Last Trump, wear a blue suit and a hat out-of-doors—leather is just allowable—remarry only older women, not gorgeous chicks; know a Royal, and keep a few Viscounts to flash at dinner in the Hilton; expose your ears, don't veil them with hair; join a lot of worthy, boring societies, particularly the Rotarians; have a yacht when you can afford it; and don't get a reputation as a writer of controversial articles that question the legitimacy or respectability of any institution, temporal or moral. Remember that the slightest tremor of change in the environment is seismically recorded by Wall Street. And the new necromancers, the analysts, will peer into your guts, not a freshly-slaughtered chicken's, if something goes wrong with your company's quotation because of you.

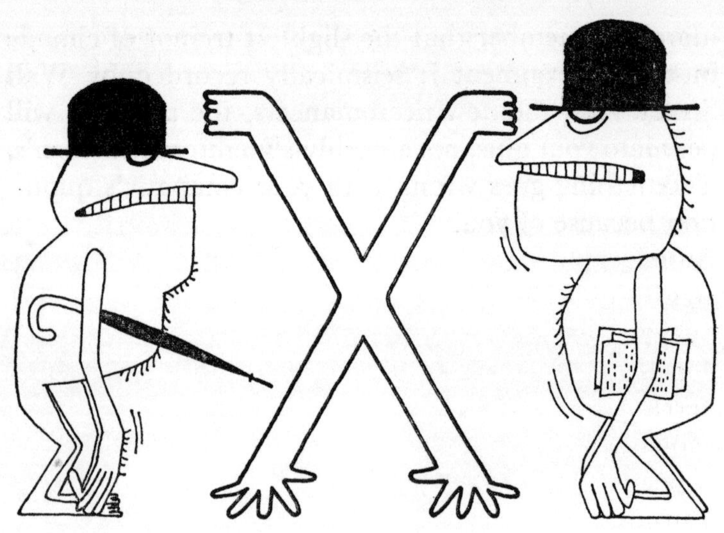

## XENOPHOBIA

Once I was showing a party of Russians over a pharmaceutical factory. A small, weasel-eyed Professor continually asked questions which slowed down the pace of the tour; finally the leader of the party, a well-known Soviet academician, drew me aside and said coldly, 'Sir, it is not necessary to show such consideration to this professor. He is from Outer Mongolia.' Families often hate their next door neighbours. Villages conspire against the loathsome people over the hill in the next hamlet. Londoners dislike Mancunians, and vice versa. Flemings plant bombs on Walloon war memorials, and Irish Catholics blow up Irish Protestant electricity offices.

Inbuilt in every human being is an insanely rapid little computer which was designed hundreds of thousands of years ago for the savage, to tell him the instant another man broke cover on the edge of the forest what was different and potentially dangerous about the new arrival. As the Nazi era showed so clearly, under the thin crust of civilisation of the last mere two thousand years, lightly slumbers the wild animal of the last million. Suspicion, hate and instant aggression were the reflexes on which tribal society survived. We see such societies in action whenever a former Colonial power withdraws from one of its ex-territories; it is only a matter of time before some violent convulsions occur because the idea of tolerating a peaceable Opposition is difficult enough for Western Europeans. And nearly impossible for those who have not had centuries of practice.

If therefore you are a Scot; or a Jew; or an Ulster-man; or a naturalised Italian or indeed from Norfolk when your chairman comes from Hampstead, remember that you may rub along marvellously for years until the day that something really goes wrong. Then he will say, 'It's so like a Scotsman to cave in when the sledding gets really tough,' or 'The Jewish race has spent the last few thousand years just staying alive in a hostile environment. You can't expect them to be brave in adversity as well,' or 'The Wogs can always be relied on to run at the sight of cold steel.'

There is not much you can do about it if you were born with a skin that was yellow, brown or burnt sienna; or if your mother decided to procreate in Bang-kok or Fiji; or your father to rear you in Argentina or Newfoundland. But just remember that, in spite of demulcent hippie cries of peace to all men, liberals opening their arms to their black brothers, and parlia-ments ruling against discrimination, human nature has dictated that the man from the next tribe is a potential threat, and under the worst strains even the perfectly adjusted manager may remember that you are not a trusted member of his own tribe.

## *YOUTH*

A new racialism is burgeoning around the world. It is the real dislike of young people for older ones and vice versa. Its cause is the pace of development—cultural, sexual, technological, artistic—so that a forty year old may easily stand back bewildered or disgusted at the activities and antics of people half his age; whereas the young—as the *Oz* trial showed so clearly—will feel that oldies posture as listening to them but in reality are deaf and forever uncomprehending.

The danger here to the Looker Behind is that all younger men are likely to think that he is a fool or a twit. And they may be creeping up on him with such hostility and in such numbers that his 'Et tu, Brute?' will have to be in sextuplicate. The best remedy is the obvious one: avoid unnecessary emphasis of the generation gap by letting your hair grow a little from the short back and sides inculcated in the last war by your sergeant major. Brace yourself to go to the wild theatrical romps that lead taste for the moment. Do something that the young recognise as tough, worth-while and essentially youthful—imagine what an effect it had on the young following of Edward Heath when his plump, comfortable figure suddenly began to be shown wrestling steely-wristed with the helms of expensive and fast racing yachts. Drive a car with a touch of devilment about it. Do not wear only your Tanks Corps tie. Instead of calling your secretary 'dear' in an off-handed asexual way that makes her feel that you are her great-uncle, fix her with a limpid stare that makes it clear that you are still dangerous. Have oddments of decoration in your office that show a little more flexibility and awareness than prints by Tretchikoff or flights of perspective ceramic duck. Come to work by different routes. Do not always entertain just in top peoples' gorging establishments. Think about the problems of the young—born into a world where every worthwhile career summit is beginning to look unclimbably vast (and many of them dull as well); where unavoidable genetic mediocrity is at a real disadvantage; where increasingly, everything novel—hair length, beards, body exposure, art forms, speed records, Everest climbs—has not only been done before, but was done again as recently as last year. It is this hopelessness, this feeling that a young man will live and die in an uninspiring anonymity that makes youth leaders like the egregious Cohn-Bendit say of society, 'Let us first destroy it, then we will talk of what we are going to build in its place.'

If you can go at least halfway to meet the really

young people in your office, you can create among them a phalanx of allies that, despite their junior rank, can get you the desirably life-preserving reputation of being like Coriolanus, beloved of the people.

## ZOOLOGY

You may not realise it, but at the cellular level we are walking zoological museums. Millions of years of slow development ever since the amoeba have been stored up in us, and any one of these saecular strata of instincts may assert itself at an unexpected time. To the would-be survivor some are much more important than others, and it is only common sense to remember the strength of these unreasoning drives in those around and above you. Status is one. In a big organisation, when executives from different sections meet, there is usually an uncomfortable canine-snuffing-round period while the two executives concerned establish who is top dog. You lose nothing in the long run by letting the other man feel superior; in fact, you probably gain because he will subsequently be more expansive in your presence. Similarly, if you seem to be dethroning your chairman by ignoring him, eroding his authority or mockingly opposing him, he will hit back as a threatened animal always does. So it does no harm to let him feel like the boss.

If two executives fall for the same secretary, no holds whatever will be barred. It is not for nothing that the old adage has arisen about all being fair in love and war.

Older men are naturally afraid of the threat of being supplanted by younger men in business as elsewhere, so that if you are ten years or more his junior remember that your boss may be one of those who gets apoplectic about the misdeeds of the younger generation not because he disapproves on rational grounds, but because he is afraid of the idea of being overtaken and swamped by the young technocratic hordes.

Nearly all normal men have latent tendencies to both persecution complexes and manic depressive behaviour. The former is important because if a man feels that he is cornered or being unfairly treated, he may have a fairly acute episode of paranoia and get both dangerous and unpleasant. And the second because, if you correctly diagnose your boss as being inclined to moods swinging between wild elation and sadness, make sure that, if possible, you time requests or misdeeds for the man's air-walking elated phase. The obsessive compulsive psychological type is a more thorny problem to deal with. In time of fear and doubt, he will do *anything* in the maddest detail because some activity, even if senseless and self-defeating is better than nothing. Excessively severe potty training, too much single-sex education at a public school, or nasty experiences like narrow escapes from the gas chambers, can all induce unreasoning guilt in man which will cause the generation of grotesque burdens of reassuring work when crisis strikes. It is the more dignified homologue of the well-known jingle:

> In any time of fear and doubt
> Shriek and yell and rush about,

but unfortunately, it is just as difficult for would-be survivors to live with compulsive overworkers as it is for stiff upper-lipped Britons to tolerate the Mediterranean-bred sailors who push women and children out of lifeboats during disasters. Sooner or later you have to cry halt to the generation of paper; or go mad yourself.

Some men are born a few drinks under par; in order for their imaginations to revolve at sufficient speed, they need alcohol. Some brains need adrenalin, and the owners of them go to great lengths to generate the necessary excitement to get this precious amine into the blood in stirring volumes. They may, for example, systematically start late for every appointment so that they have to drive like the wind of death to make it on time. Or quarrel excitingly with their colleagues at meetings. Or throw histrionics about their principles or the threats to them from competitors. If your boss is such a person, you must remember that nothing will change in him as the years go by. In fact he will get worse. So that, if his behaviour upsets you beyond bearing, you will be well advised to take the *Daily Telegraph* on Fridays from now on.

Generally speaking, if you observe your dog closely, his behaviour is largely applicable to that of your boss. A discreet pat is usually appreciated, even if modestly disclaimed. A regular good meal is a must. The barking ecstasy of 'Walkies' may be translated to a good weekly sales-to-budget performance. A comfortable office hung with panoply is a good dog bed with a few favourite dog toys, shinbones and so on. Avoiding his direct gaze makes him feel more at ease. Sudden noises (particularly from the board or shareholders) alarm him, and may trigger some incoherent motor activity. And, under circumstances of real tension—being held back from a bitch on heat, for example, or tormented by over-stimulation—he may forget who is friend and who is enemy.